How Toys Work

Screws, Nuts, and Bolts

Siân Smith

www.raintreepublishers.co.uk
Visit our website to find out more information about Raintree books.

To order:
☎ Phone 0845 6044371
▤ Fax +44 (0) 1865 312263
▣ Email myorders@raintreepublishers.co.uk

Customers from outside the UK please telephone +44 1865 312262

Raintree is an imprint of Capstone Global Library Limited, a company incorporated in England and Wales having its registered office at 7 Pilgrim Street, London, EC4V 6LB – Registered company number: 6695582

Text © Capstone Global Library Limited 2013
First published in hardback in 2013
First published in paperback in 2014
The moral rights of the proprietor have been asserted.

Edited by Dan Nunn, Rebecca Rissman, and Sian Smith
Designed by Joanna Hinton-Malivoire
Picture research by Mica Brancic
Production by Victoria Fitzgerald
Originated by Capstone Global Library Ltd
Printed in China

ISBN 978 1 4062 3801 3 (hardback)
16 15 14 13 12
10 9 8 7 6 5 4 3 2 1

ISBN 978 1 4062 3808 2 (paperback)
17 16 15 14 13
10 9 8 7 6 5 4 3 2 1

British Library Cataloguing in Publication Data
Smith, Sian.
 Screws, nuts, and bolts. -- (How toys work)
 1. Screws--Juvenile literature. 2. Bolts and nuts--Juvenile literature.
 I. Title II. Series
 621.8'82-dc22

Acknowledgements
The author and publisher are grateful to the following for permission to reproduce copyright material: © Capstone Global Library Ltd pp.8, 17, 22b (Lord and Leverett); © Capstone Publishers pp.6, 7 main, 9 inset, 9 main, 12, 13, 14, 15, 18, 19, 21, 10 inset, 10 main, 11 inset, 23 top (Karon Dubke); Shutterstock pp. 20, 5 (© Noam Armonn), 7 inset (© HomeStudio), 16 (© sonya etchison), 22a (© Nelstudio), 22c (© John Kasawa), 22d (© Tish1), 23 bottom (© HomeStudio), 23 middle bottom (© Jaroslaw Grudzinski), 23 middle top (© Taurus), 4 bottom left (© studio BM), 4 bottom right (© thirayut), 4 top left (© Piotr Sikora), 4 top right (© Noah Golan).

Cover photograph of toys made out of nuts and bolts reproduced with permission of Shutterstock (© Gary Blakeley). Back cover photograph of a spanner being used on a nut reproduced with permission of © Capstone Publishers (Karon Dubke).

We would like to thank David Harrison, Nancy Harris, Dee Reid, and Diana Bentley for their assistance in the preparation of this book.

Every effort has been made to contact copyright holders of material reproduced in this book. Any omissions will be rectified in subsequent printings if notice is given to the publisher.

Contents

Different toys

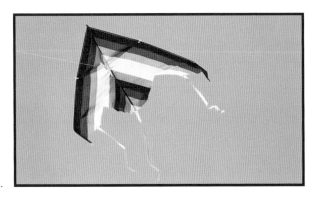 

There are many different kinds
of toys.

Toys work in different ways.

Screws

screws

Some toys use screws.

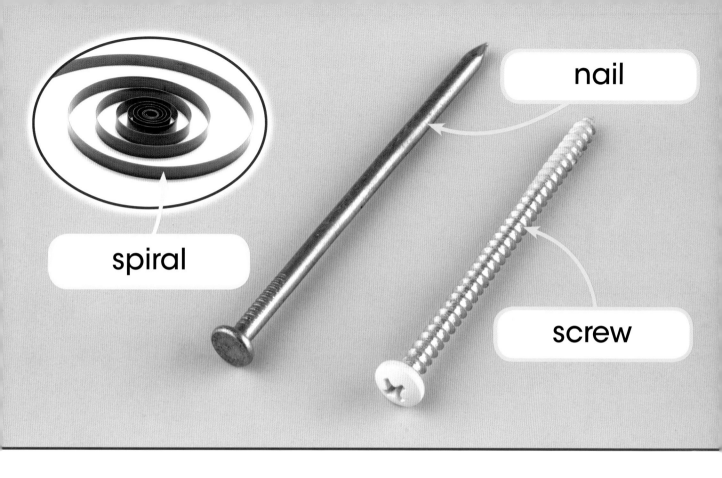

spiral

nail

screw

A screw is like a nail with a spiral around it.

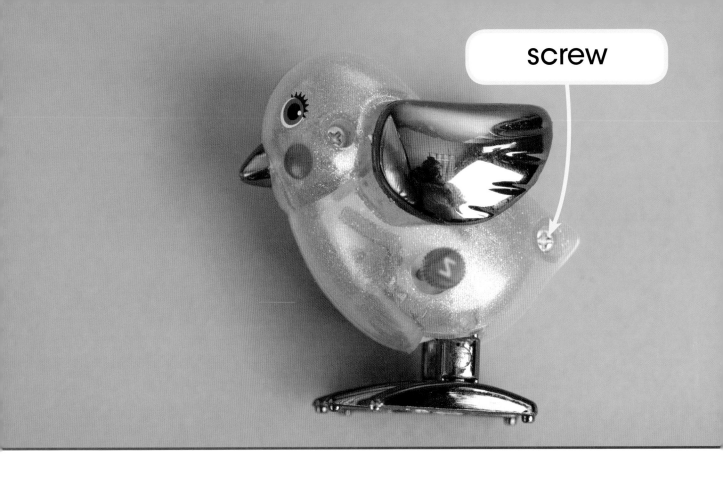

screw

We use screws to hold things together.

spiral

screw

The spiral on a screw makes it hard to pull out.

Screws hold this car together.

Screws hold this computer game together.

Nuts and bolts

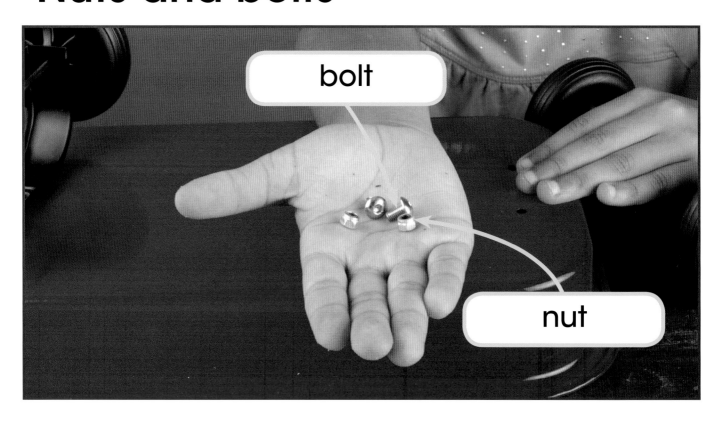

bolt

nut

Some toys use nuts and bolts.

Nuts and bolts hold things together,
too.

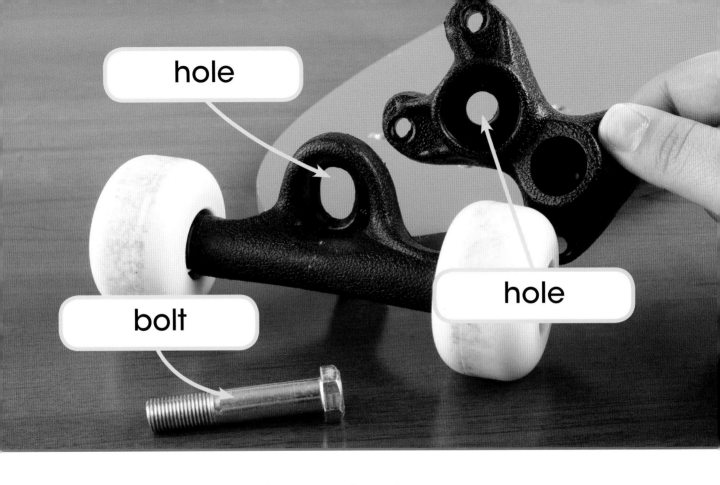

hole

hole

bolt

Two pieces have holes.

A bolt goes through the holes.

nut

A nut goes on the end of the bolt.
It holds the pieces together.

nut and bolt

Nuts and bolts hold this climbing
frame together.

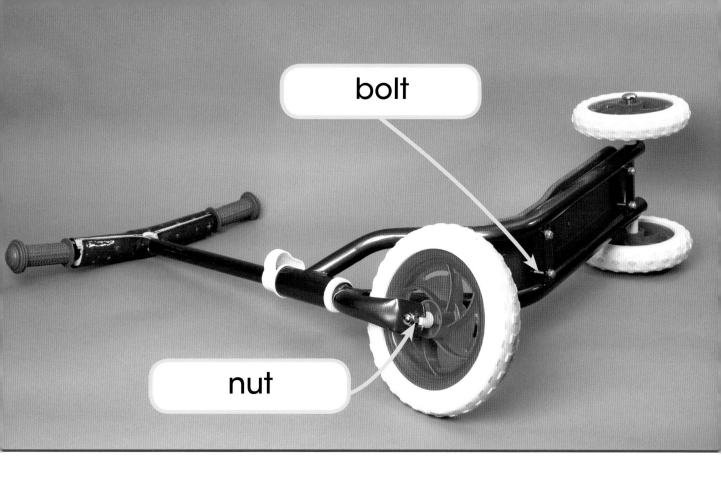

bolt

nut

Nuts and bolts hold this scooter together.

Turning

We have to turn a screw to push it in.

We have to turn a screw to pull it out.

We have to turn a nut to put it on a bolt.

screwdriver

We use a screwdriver to turn a screw.

spanner

We use a spanner to turn a nut.

Quiz

(a)

(b)

(c)

(d)

Which one of these toys uses screws?

Answer on page 24

Picture glossary

bolt a kind of thick screw with a flat end

nut a small piece of metal or plastic with a hole in it

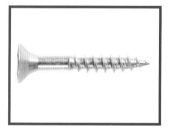
screw a thin, pointed piece of metal similar to a nail. A screw has a spiral around it.

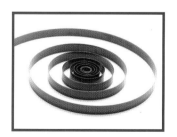
spiral a shape like a curl that winds round and round

Index

Answer to question on page 22: Toy b uses screws.

Notes for parents and teachers

Introduction

Show the children a collection of screws, nails, nuts, and bolts. Select children to pick out a screw, a nail, a nut, and a bolt. Label one example of each together. What similarities and differences can they find between the nail, the screw, and the bolt? What do we use these things for?

More information about screws, nuts, and bolts

Explain that screws and bolts are different to nails because they have a spiral (or helix) shape around the outside. On a screw this is called the thread. The thread on a screw means that you have to turn the screw to put it in something or take it out. A bolt is like a thicker screw and most bolts have flat ends. Children can look at the thread on the end of a bolt and the thread inside a nut, and see how a nut can be put on a bolt to hold things in place.

Follow up activities

Give the children the opportunity to experience how screws, nuts, and bolts can be used to hold things together. They could build or take apart models using a construction set. Show them how to use a screwdriver and spanner safely. For more advanced work on simple machines, children can work with an adult to discuss and play the games at: www.edheads.org/activities/simple-machines

24